THE
INVISIBLE
WORLD

POEMS

MATT DALY

For information contact:
Unsolicited Press
Portland, Oregon
www.unsolicitedpress.com
orders@unsolicitedpress.com
619-354-8005

Cover Design: Kathryn Gerhardt
Editor: S.R. Stewart

ISBN: 978-1-963115-07-9

Introduction

This book began as a conversation with a single, troubling and troublesome ancestor.

My lineage links back to the Mather family, prominent Puritans from the early colonial period, who helped set the course toward many of the destructive and shameful practices that Anglo-American culture has enacted on people and ecosystems around the world. Since discovering this lineage, I have felt a sense that I needed to address it in some way, not to redress its wrongs but at least to face them in the hope of making sense of how I might live outside of their influence.

I thought reading the writings of the Mathers, to look into the evidence of their thinking and rhetoric, would be a reasonable place to start. When I went looking into the work of Increase and Cotton Mather, I was quickly drawn to a text by Cotton Mather with a title I found unexpectedly beautiful: *The Wonders of the Invisible World*. But I did not find beauty in his work.

Mather's version of "wonders" primarily involves elucidating the ways the Devil inhabits wild places and the people, especially women, who approach or engage with these places. Mather saw wildness as the habitat for evil, linking who and what lived there to Satan. The American continent was cast as a place to be purged of its darkness. This rhetoric sounded alarmingly familiar.

And so, I created a daily practice of reading sections of *The Wonders of the Invisible World* and writing responses to what I found there. In the beginning, I had thought that this work would move into an investigation of gender and race and power and my own complicity in systems of dominance. However, in responding to Mather's wonders, I kept gravitating to my sense of good and right, and how to live well with others, as arising in and from the rural and wild places where I have lived and with the people I have known and loved in these places.

My responses to Mather made me think about ancestry and how the origins of the word "ancestor" have to do with going before. This investigation has led me to a sense of ancestry as the connections to people with whom I have lived in and near wild places, people who have gone before me and led the way into living lands that I love.

I have tried to make the compromised intimacy of a life in love with places that still hold some remaining wildness and the inhabitants of these places visible in the hope of healing some small wound among the injuries wrought by my ancestry, my ancestor's voice, and what has followed from his voice.

Acknowledgements

I am thankful to the editors of the following publications in which several of these poems have previously appeared: *Panhandler Magazine, Red Ogre Review,* and *Stand Magazine.*

Many thanks to Summer Stewart for her enthusiasm, guidance and editorial expertise as well as to the entire Unsolicited Press team for shepherding so many good books into the world.

I am grateful to family, friends, and fellow poets who have offered love, care and honest critique about the poems and everything else. I love you.

I also offer gratitude to each of the people referred to in this collection as "ancestors" and to the more-than-human beings in conversation with us and to the places we all inhabit and without which we would be lost.

Poems

THE
INVISIBLE
WORLD

POEMS

THE WONDER IS LAND

I have never nearly died in a storm.   Of course, my ancestor, there have been blizzards, even one summer whiteout, into which I disappeared, but then time keeps merely passing until I warm back up.   Sometimes I think terrible things are just waiting to pour down on me, and other times I imagine the worst for the people I love and then myself long-suffering.   It's terrible, but I do not stop.   Like every sky, I am not without others, and like air so cold it is almost not atmosphere, I am always in the sky just here above me.

Before you begin, my ancestor, build yourself a barricade dimensioned in diameters for stockade or for pyre.   You cannot choose your blood, but you can select your fury.   You are the father who works in secret inside me.   What is inside your code is still in my makeup: the fury and the self-righteousness of flames.   I have no clawhammer or pry bar but the type-set tools you've offered me to begin the tearing down.   I have no lieutenant governor to justify my observance of the rule or its exception.   The spirits I see around me and feel inside my lungs, are, I think, the same spirits you were eager to docket for a trial.   My sun emerges watery from winter clouds as just a sphere of light for what grows from its own cells.   What I worship never had a name or a place in your endeavors.   You can't imagine I've seen what I've seen.   And not just because you are dirt again or trapped within neatly piled stones.   You are the ember I can't extinguish.   You are the flicker I can't help but stoke just so the source of a river I've been to many times can snuff out the ether

1

you breathed, the mark you made that no roots in my flesh ever wanted to draw into the warp of their fibers or the ink-and-lead marks on their unlimited-as-the-living-world skin.

My ancestor, you whet your lead blade to furrow where forests used to be.   Your sermon has only ever been about the ladder-pyre built sheaf upon sheaf from the skeletons of hardwoods and other wild bones.   Upon hearing anyone but yourself whisper, you spread the soot ink, sharpen the ax-tongue of voice, the quill feather of a forgotten waterfowl.

I write my name into the earth's parchment unfolding unevenly in all directions around my trammeled heart.   I use for a stylus a gnarled stick broken from a sagebrush.   It is August, my birth month, and there is a highway because, these days, we are never without such unintelligible circumstances as a barrier that is also a way through.   An army of carrion and a confederacy of plastic sacks and bottles from factory foods breaks in upon the rockchips and cursive tar.   Vultures drift in their lopsided spirals like angels on the lookout for the trumpets they don't want anyone to notice they have misplaced.   They tuck their earthworm heads into their cowls.   Crows and magpies make one ring.   Cowbirds another.   Ravens refuse the hierarchy of wait and meat.   One golden eagle rises from a struck fawn.   The cell rot of the updraft breaks in, and the spiral I sketch into the sand falters and wobbles.   I understand that the world you found, my ancestor, gave death more often as a gift than the world I now encounter.   I understand that you wanted the world to remake itself into a smelted place without so many losses, and you were willing to sacrifice some gains, such as the pulsing self and a place beyond what can grow outside the head.   I see how you fashioned yourself as the overseer, the virgin birth of the voice against mischief.   How you swatted a cry from vellum bound in a thicker skin.   I see how easy it is to forget the days before I knew how to write a word that would never leave me alone, a rude neighbor causing all the other residents, who have been here longer than the notion of Halcyon, to keep their distance as best they can from our shadowed doors.

Not yet has a churchlight converted me, not even evening's rapt passage through the alabaster panes in the Orvieto Duomo, which is nearly enough to make what we make seem sacred, but once I heard a river say something I could not quite make out.   When I asked, "What?" and again, "What?", all the river did was keep on talking.   I approached on my knees, at least, if not precisely penitent.   The passage from glacier to surfmist had finned the bedrock limestone into leaves and holed one fin for midday to pass through and through the skin of the water and the flesh of the water and through whatever in me passes for spirit until the light and the soft green wavering below everything wavered.   Here in the afternoon of who I am, I spend more time inside than out, but the wild light which has placed itself upon me is still almost like a voice inside which goes on saying something nearly, if not quite, aloud.

There was a ridge above the camp where I slept most nights that first summer I was almost a man.   I bathed naked in the creek and let mosquitoes feed until my skin refused to be bumped by them.   I had no itch beyond the animal hungers.   Workdays, I counted sprouts of pines and firs and other plants where a year before was fire and char.   I wore

3

black between finger and nail, knuckle creases cartooned with soot.   But none of this is about the ridge where I hiked when I went where I wanted or the Douglas fir that towered there or how the hand of many fires had held the trunk by the waist and leaned in to kiss a scar.   Scar after scar and still the tree towered above me and the ridge and the lichened limestone and the biting flies driven past by the ridgewind.   I slid my hands into the smooth wood folds surrounded by the thickness of corklike bark and felt how smooth we are left after the spark of rock on rock or lightning reaching down.   I felt in my polished self the woody wildness that in these intervening years has never lost its grain nor has it ever gnarled.

That first evening I ran into the storm I carried: a blanket, my wet hair, nothing else.   What I ran from is lost and must have something to do with love and was not the storm.   It was evening and the sky was like the sea beyond the surf, like the space inside my mouth, full of winged things and bits of plants that seemed like wings pushed around in the wind.   I ran to the fenceline and sat at the border between the comfortable sadness and the open field.   I did not know your prayers, my ancestor, and did not care to say one.   My mother called and I returned to her.   Maybe she came to me as the first drops slapped the frogs quiet.   Maybe I am still the same person.   The tides inside me that night boom around the valley.   I still feel safe in the rain.   The world has no need for churches.

The shard that stuck inside my finger beside the pointer knuckle was flecked with shimmer.   I broke rocks from the yard all summer just to see what sparkled them.   Sometimes the hammer shanked, and sparks flashed and fell.   Blood welled from where the shard entered.   For years, beneath the scar I could find a knot of what might have been a part of a mountain.   When I reflect on what I can remember, I feel the world around me and inside me erode to *cleave* and *cleave to*.   Beside the river, I toss broken cobbles back into the wear-down water.   Although you and I seem like shards, there are reasons men like us listen and even borrow both *roll* and also *tumble*.

I don't remember precisely how you and I became blood brothers, my ancestor, so let's say we used the pocketknife I'd found in the outfield, and let's say we opened our palms and pressed them together in the decadent willows behind your trailer house.   Those willows that, if we could find how they opened, held inside a little space for shelter.   Let's say we sucked stems and missed magpies with our BB shots, and then just stopped and slit ourselves open to one another.   Let's say I felt the crowd of blood cells dodging each other on the way into and out of the places in us that would later never become office parks.   Let's say, my ancestor, that we were constantly happy with our country situation as boys somewhere green and small.   Let's admit we never bothered with the viewsheds so much of the world now sees in advertisements for mid-sized SUVs, because the small places were portioned just so to fit us into them, to stain our bodies and to be stained.   Let's talk about how you became a civil engineer with only a minor stint as a drinking problem.   That might let me admit how nice whiskey feels inside when I'm alone.   Let's say how long our blood ran together even after we were old enough to have nothing in common.   Let's mention the place, the pointless rural situation where we grew up

5

together, that still runs through us although it's all mansions now and conservation easements and roads too narrow for the flow of summer cars.   We could even bring up how none of this was quite true or at least accurate or ever ours to begin with.

                    First a rifting in the creekbank, then we took to   our   hands   and   tore,   badger-like,   the   creekbank down.   Steers followed as they always follow until their bravest chuffed and we turned and rose and chuffed back and sent them scampering and mud-sculpting our teardown work to soft loss of form to the creekbank we tore down.   Given summer heat, we'd rend whatever we could rend.   Given winter the steers were meat and eaten and the snow piled its bulwarks on our handiwork and the world for the cold passage did not feel at all like our cruel domain to reign our liberty upon it.

                    My ancestor, you splayed your hands across a space in a split granite chunk both the size and shape of a hayloaf we'd never pitch flakes from down to the cattle herding below.   No ranchwork had shaped our shoulders.   Your gecko-wide fingerpads gripped the stippled stone.   I followed your ease with my clumsiness and fear until we both squatted ape-like on the bouldertop and watched the scree field mirror the stormclouds gathering Augustward and my departure from this brotherhood that had not yet turned to anything desperate or other than between boys.   I trembled.   Afternoon warmed the way down toward the slow igneous cascade toward glaciermelt to   named   stream   to   levee-bound   river   coursing   near   our homes.   My time was coming to hem in.   You scrambled your scramble down while I scooted ignobly on my bellyflesh,   scoured   by   pricks   of   rock   until   I   rashed   and bled.   You were never one to laugh at my faults.   You waited while I shamed myself uninjured and muttering to meet you.   The valley formed into cloudless haze paused before predictable flashes and resonance from what humidity built up on the ridgelines.   Already, I was vaporlike and already frozen and far off and lifting from the crashing surf and a solitude that for years would cling to me.

          We stomped small feet, waiting for the bus to take us to school.   All of us, even you, familiar with this: mist latched to branch and post but not to wire.   The wire dragon-crackled on our frozen road.   We bigger kids circled the younger as bison bodily pen their young from wolves.   The dragon wire sparked, and we stomped the little ones' curiosity for the blue sparks on the white road.   When the bus rose yellow through the day's frozen gray, we let the driver thunder out to us, "Stay back," but none of us fool enough to think the sky or what fell from the sky might send us beyond our raising.   Not even you, my ancestor, departed our animal circle, stomping and breathing out our animal noses in our animal circle.   Even young, we knew, as we want all the young to know without a word, that it is what we make beginning with what charge we raise between frozen ground and frost above that will stop us beat and breath when winter snaps the cords we string or tie.   Our little feet yet not ready.

          Crescent after crescent shook in the leaf dapple before totality chilled the space we breathed.   The shielding and then, when the moon thumbed the sun away and we could look uncluttered by old visions at what the rays might hollow out in our peering, we looked.   The space between us and the moon, then the space between that gray lump and our star, then us and that fusion, then us and the confusion of the other visible suns became, simply and for the first time, an interdependency of spaces.   As clearly as the distance shivering between leaves, I grasped into a grasping and the branching out of the thoughts I can't help but think make me, and I let go of the last spent leaf of any belief in any mind perfect enough to make not words, or things but that betweenesses everywhere between us, you and me, my ancestor.

I have not seen lightning strike a tree, a subalpine fir like you saw once in a storm.   You claimed the trunk glowed for a moment then burst apart.   I was there just after the squall calmed or moved on and simply stood still to witness the uncharred shards, all those spears of blond wood still wet with the striving of cells.   What I have seen, in fact nearly been knocked down by, is wind.   Not any special gust built up from currents warmed by our coals in the exhausted gulf, but the steady blow across the inland.   I tried to stand near the overcast river, the edge willows doubled over as if bowed, but the empty strength of air took my feet, dusted with broken snow crystals, and sent me where it willed, which is, of course, always along its scour.   I washed up against the ice-rimed shallows before fighting my way back to the truck, the road striking the high steppe in its plain violence.

Between two houses: cottonwoods and pasture, sere field and a seep.   At your house, my ancestor, a mother who peered and smoked through a magnifying glass armature to paint watercolors of river cobbles she'd lugged home from her levee walks with her salt-and-pepper bouviers.   At my house, silence and a hall.   Your stepfather quiet and maybe already drunk and far down among brass casings and sounds.   My stepfather on horseback or barned with his hands.   The afternoon wind rattling thistleheads and kicking up the grasshoppers we kicked up on our way to the swamp partway between where our houses stayed, where we mucked and leapt, frogged and leeched, forgot that the sun spotted my father into divot scars, sprang blond-legged over the tannic water sometimes softbanked into the muck and eggs as if each canyon gust could tumble us my way or your way to the barbed-wire creek or a box of matches and soldiers to try to launch by bottlerocket anyplace else or to make a scene, strike and melt into one another.

                    We lived where once lived a wicked river taking time to move stones among stones, lift and let go of trees, carve eddies and braids.   All the living things, even me and you, my ancestor, moving in the wicked river.   Then your father and other men quarried and, as men do, piled stones along the riverbank, turning that once wicked river into something tamer and more turbulent.   Two girls from our subdivision had a father who drowned in that diked river fetching a lure for a fisherman.   That was the first time I understood how a father could wake up in the same house and then later be gone.   Now I am a father and you, my ancestor, were at the oars when a man sprung from your raft when it struck a dike stone.   You rowed and rowed after the sinking man whose eyes never closed the whole time he was drowning, but the river and the man together fled you.   I have known wickedness and even death, and I have also known the river and its waters almost as well as I have ever known anyone I might call *ancestor*.

                    We marched through waves of white crystals altaring the trail to mud and then to gone.   The world went black and white while we marched on.   We stopped near where you said there was a lake.   All I could do was trust your broad hands and help pitch the tent.   We slept the storm into an invitation for passing.   We woke into a tabernacle of drifts, a black lake and ridges that now seem like jawline flesh.   The whole if it felt made for us, made by us and ready to forget our passage.   We gave ourselves to wanderlust and have not stopped.   Like winter, our bodies' stillness is not the same as giving up.   We are still like swans trumpeting whitely ahead of our wings into a bright sky free of the golden figure if not its light.   My ancestor, you taught me to have faith in my animal self like a question currents of air answer into melt.

You leaned into summer. my ancestor, and became nothing so alive as summer after the balsamroot gives the hillsides back to sage.   The boy you were with when you discovered how easily two machine-made things, a rope and a harness, can remain apart from one another said he would return to that cliffrock band but not before the passing of more than one more rain.   He was a stranger to me, and you were just a girl I barely knew then, my ancestor, when I was old enough to be a father but not yet one.   You remain the difference between washing away and soaking in, falling apart and a part falling, even now falling.

Most of all this was in a time when the river carried fewer people and the dike which held the river in check held the feet of fewer people and their dogs.   Imagine again your mother there with both of her bouviers: the dogs trotting and sniffing and shaggy, your mother gathering cobbles to later watercolor under a magnifying glass with a brush so thin I thought it held just one hair, the precision and the imprecision of the land.　　　Imagine her leaving us near the highway bridge, driving the dike down to the green metal gate where she would meet us hours later.　　　Imagine the sun angling a little more toward winter and us first on the cobble islands and then in the water.　　　We had no raft but simply our boy bodies and sometimes a cottonwood snag to offer the current.　　　We gasped and our blood adjusted, and we floated over schools of whitefish until our shivering drew us back to the dry islands and the first golden leaves.　　　Another passage from the world into our own world with what was left of the wild around us.　　　Now that you, my ancestor, are far to the west and drawing blood in an urban place, and I have all but forgotten your face, the currents pull us still.　　　When another, much-later vision of you, my ancestor, oared a raft into the riprap currents and a man flew against the rocks and then into the water, you said the drowning man never closed his eyes.　　　I don't let go of the smooth stones much these days, but I can't help but feel the currents lifting and not lifting all around me.

　　　Remember us, my ancestor, on one side of a trail bridge, a dude wrangler slouched aback his horse, the other.　　　Between icemelt roaring and four tourists left to themselves to cross the high planks over white water.　　　The kids already out of their saddles.　　　Father and horse skidded obliquely to the edge and then somehow just the horse went over.　　　The guide lazed the far bank.　　　The horse kicked half upside down in the water.　　　The kids made sounds like piteous squeals or laughter.　　　We stood a while, silent, and went on.　　　The problems made by unmoved men on one side and on the other the horse's fate uncertain.　　　We kept in motion as if not already also unmade by water.

The gracious presence in the midst of me is the lost ghost of an animal in an unseen swale, shaped by equal parts mist and traitorous dust.　　　　What pricked its ears listened.　　　　What prowled for blood or sought nectar thirsted.　　　　What died at our hands rose as vellum.　　　　I have no prayers.　　　　I do not plan to be stripped of my gristle.　　　　What lies in the nest of my chest, the den within, is animal and breathes in the voice of an animal.

　　　　　　　　　　　You and I played a game called "Slit the Devil's Throat."　　　　First, find a few flat cobbles; the best ones are worn smooth.　　　　Hold as many as you can in your off hand.　　　　Next, step close to the wavelets nudging driftwood and leaves toward the spidered shore.　　　　Stand beside me, my ancestor, almost brushing shoulders as if close could be the same as stable or not losing your balance.　　　　Tossing techniques vary.　　　　Overhand works if you pitch the angle high.　　　　Underhand gets good spin but if your grip is tight can send your stone above your heads instead of lakeward.　　　　Throw as high as you can so that the stone falls straight as a diver toward the water and like a diver splits the water from the water almost soundlessly.　　　　Little splash and little sound.　　　　In the hospital on the day you gasped and puffed into your first dreams alive in dry country, you said, "Your job is to let go of me," as softly as erosion.　　　　One by one pluck a stone from your off hand and send it above, which is simply another way of saying into the green depth, *As long as I can hold bits of peaks for you, I will hold them.*　　　　I am holding my breath now for as long as it takes to let the wet stones dry, the tokens you drew from the shallows where the waves gestured them, into muted shades secreting briefly their full colors from that terrible summer heat above them.

We camped in a gas field shaled over green water already reaching for and never reaching the Pacific. We calmed despite the clank of a well's unrelenting. We followed a wash fuzzed with ants toward the willows by the river, the boulders in the cliffs eroded by the old forces, older than fear. The boulders gave way to a sandstone canvas carved in both the likely beauty and the need for naming. Here a tendril-limbed figured, there two letters in equation with two other letters bordered by a heart-shaped scratch in the stained membrane of the long-ago contours of an inland sea. You and I passed the honor and defacement in search of the petroglyph we'd come to see: a line of mounted figures impossibly large and hopelessly charging a train. Mosquitos droned. The wells kept on turning the earth inside out. Gusts off the downstream bends scoured the rock face imperceptibly and always. I hid deeply, but not quite from myself, the lesson of unlearning, that terrible gift that people give just this: not learning.

The return down-canyon and the surface skimmed by wind into a pattern made of surrounding shapes but without the bulk of their scoured and unscoured surfaces. You and I encountered a man who said he always walked around clockwise because of the prettier views. We passed him near the western shore scummed with something the wind had carried there, a film pressed against the sand. Our walk took us the other way to where the mirrored center of the lake held. The lesser ridges we love most on the opposite side of the valley defined themselves with snow. All summer, wildfire smoke haze stained the far ridges into plainness. Lake, sky and ridgeline composed themselves. My ancestor, your injury has healed to what is now your full capacity. You are doing the inner work to live as well as you can with the other people you must live with.   Times have come and gone when we were not sure that we liked each other, but we kept meeting on an up-and-back trail or a loop.   My awareness of my faults and failings, like a haze in me that a walk in a wild place with my ancestor almost, if not completely, clears coldly to bright.

                              I stood once in a river where a hot spring met the glacial race away to its engulfment so that one foot numbed while the other flared.   This is an ordinary place visited by the uncounted and the counted.   The spring fell from a head-high drop and behind its plummet, a mist-enshrouded hollow steamed like the inside of a lung.   The cost of passage from wide sky to this close place was a breath and the drum weight of water stumbling me.   Inside, a loud world without shadows.   The relief of shadowlessness held me.   I didn't last long in the heat of a spot of this without that.   Returning, the world held my skin with stormclouds.   Like you, my ancestor, I know those who have seen a shimmer as a veil and gone under.

                         I am still up there in the field of stones: my body, my desire for other bodies, touch, the word which fits in a box, my thumps and rattles, those of others, those of other others, abrasion, different words for *stone*, other stones.   I open my mouth and feel the old fissure, the clamber down.   I touch and am touched for abrasion and the wearing down.   When I am in the wind, there I am: an arch not a bridge.   When I stand spraddle-legged in the river, alone or beside you or crossing toward a new meadow with you in your days and nights and what is between

14

them, when I am eroded by the currents above the surface and those below, I sense myself of stone becoming mouth-shaped, the flecks of me misting and muddying to settle into malleable silt and dune.   These days, when I speak, the box falls apart and what has been compacted runs rewilded and loose.

                    The first time you and I slept together, my ancestor, in the truck parked not far from a river, you woke up laughing, and the star-dappled lateness of your giddiness darkened me.   No clouds passed blackly between you and the sinuous appendage of stars.   Your soot dog needed to be lifted front first and then back end into the pop-up camper in the bed of the truck where I did not help, instead forming a ridge of my body to split the valley of my night from you.   We share a way of centering ourselves in the wild woods that is a release from centers, and on that night our similarity made me jealous of you, so I pretended to sleep, and you made believe I was a stone.   For as long as I can remember birds, I remember feeling like a fool.   In the wilderness of your grace, you, my ancestor, allowed me to lose myself until I gave up losing.   The river misted and then later almost fogged, and by the time morning birdsonged over us, the river was as clear as breathing and the sky quieted and everything feathered about us ruffled.   We found fallen eggshells the color of high pressure, also nest down, and we have felt the muscles within us which, when avian, hold wings.

                    We intended to sleep in a field of fireweed stems reddening already toward fall, every leaf laden with yesterday's rain.   Our packs were heavier than necessary as is to be expected when nimble boys hike toward treeline for one night thinking how not far might mean never carry too much.　　　　Approaching a flat place and a copse of subalpine fir, we saw the first carcass of a sheep and then another and so on until the meadow filled with white tufts still awash in lanolin and not yet rot.　　　　We figured a bolt in the night had scared them dead.　　　　Somehow you knew, my ancestor, that such an end was possible, and we moved quietly higher and away from what was left.　　　　Years later, when neither of us spent much time where our mothers and stepfathers raised us or those mountains greened after the thaw, we laughed together with the women we would marry and divorce, and then you never spoke directly to me again.　　　　One more silence I can't suss out.　　　　I hear you drink too much in the time between night and morning, after almost not surviving a wreck.　　　　The sheep are so far back in time that no one thinks of that place as summer pasture.　　　　When the next storm comes, I ought to walk into what falls without my voice and with nothing on my back just to see what happens.

Of course, in this way I have loved a place enough to call it homeground, I have wanted to ember.　　　　I have stepped over snags still smoldering, branch knots whispering smoke, and I have listened to the crackle as if a language might be useful for conflagration.　　　　I have thrilled to see a run of canopy flames along a ridgeline and been ashamed after hearing no homes were lost.　　　　What I have built is not so much a life as it is a pile of sticks.　　　　Once I helped you blow a spark into charred cloth, placed the ribbon of glow into dry grass that you blew and blew until it caught.　　　　I speak and go on speaking.　　　　Once, my ancestor, you assumed that I would burn for not believing and I thought, *here I am*.　　　　What burns in me grows faint and then it heats back up.　　　　What burns in me coats my life in soot.　　　　You might see ways the world chars that I have not noticed and how, with or without us, it springs back up.

ANIMAL / ANCESTOR

Trumpeter Swans

I should tell you, my ancestor, about the first ghost who came
between us: my grandmother, your diluted blood.

She carried your artifacts, like a madness, well before her birth.

Even when her fingers were unborn wisps and the land was still
full of pigeonsong, she pressed your objects in among the rags in
her grandmother's handcart beside the smooth-triggered pistol I
fondled as a child and recast my own passage through a land of tall
grasses and bones.

On the wind, your words wore the metal down.

Across landscapes unsettled and storms beyond your governance,
the people between us traveled and plowed, built and killed as best
they could.

My grandmother — whose house was stone and whose husband
snuck out before dawn to pluck your hand-me-downs, like
sprinkler parts, from the garbage can — her ghost rose between us
in my mother's house furnished with your residue.

She was gauzy, like mist freezing by the warm spring where swans
thrive despite the oratorical drive to govern all our lives by the
discharge of gunpowder.

The swans, whose white wings never call to mind your angels,
trumpet in the midday storm without brass.

Like a devil, grandmother never tormented me.

Like the Devil, I cannot pick out her face in the lineup of faces
stretching back across the continent to your bronze shoulders.

I used to think of her as the bridge, but like the origins of rivers,
there are many springs.

Grandmother, in whom something of you never diluted or cooled,
still haunts our branch of your precious hardwood and refuses to
confess.

Unlike you, I could not pinprick the contour map of adornments
where she might end up.

Funny not to know which earth we burdened with her old hands.

We too have something molten deep within.

Her ghost was not a shade I was afraid of and so, just like that, it
left me in the dark by the front door.

I wish you could be more like her, but your voice imposed a cut
into the land which remains raised and bald and white.

About the scars on trees which look like eyes or wings, I refuse to speak with you.

About those other ghosts, the animal bodies of the pine forest that encircles me, the wild lives that passed through flesh and who will not leave me and who no longer sound, my telling bides its time.

Cliff Swallow

I can't remember when I started answering myself in another
voice, in a voice I knew was not-quite human.

I can't be sure when I began to say instead, "more-than-human,"
to turn what was animal into greater.

I can't pinpoint the day I squashed my first living thing without
saying a word, just used my skin and what is always underneath it
as a weapon.

How when I see a group of any small animals, if I think *flock*, I
think *beautiful* and if I think *swarm*, my body vireos into a vocal
hunger or iridesces swallow-like as if the cliff swallows ravenous
over the more-than-avian shimmer of the voiceless currents of the
river.

Spotted Frog

What I remember is looking up into a blue sky with a few white
clouds.

The Earth buzzed its insect buzz.

I held a clasp knife I picked up from the outfield some time
before.

(I still have the knife and have offered it to my only son.)

I pinned the frog with my weaker hand, the left one that I buried
in my mitt for the rest of the summer, the mitt that a bumble bee
stumbled into once and stung my palm, tearing itself apart to
pierce me.

The hot air stilled.

My skin burned.

My indifferent stab.

The split frog gazed up past my eyes into a space we could not
fathom and absent in noonlight of the pale grace of the Milky Way
slashing the dark.

Gray Wolf

We were driving, and there it was, my ancestor, posed in the close
corner of a ranch fence not far from a few cows: a wolf.

Not far from the highway, the wolf was unmistakable even if the
cows could care less, and the frosted barbed wires, and we did not
stop; we just kept on driving toward our comfortable home, the
four borders of a house holding familiarity if not-quite-any-longer
love.

The cows looked and lowed.

Who am I fooling?

The cows simply stood stock still.

Three cows avoided tilting their dished faces toward where the
wolf posed in the corner as if noticing how its bristling and
brindled indifference to them or fence or highway might bring
about a feral shift in one of the herd or in one of us in the car, and
the whole of this wild world might grow lanky within us and drive
us to somewhere fenceless that we didn't know or want but to
where we were already loping.

Yearling Elk

My ancestor, companion, you levered the bolt, raised the rifle
scope eyeward.

Your eyes leveled to a yearling elk still in a cold swale.

Below-zero November light filled the hillside.

Shot, impossibly, after shot filled the pocket of morning and the
elk neither fled nor fell.

So many shots another hunter shouted out, "What are you
shooting at?"

You didn't answer but bolted another bullet, impossibly, the last
shot into the chamber.

The yearling buckled but did not fall.

He stood a long time, and we waited numb from hinged bodies
and early winter.

Chilled, we stood and pressed toward the yearling until he fled.

Upslope, we trailed the red thread stitched into the crust of snow
sunslicked and frozen not-quite firm.

In a crease higher on the slope the elk bedded, we thought dying, and so we bedded again into our crouch and waited for death to make of the moment a structure of crystals that might hold our weight, but the yearling rose again, as if reborn, and moved on.

We followed tracks and blood until the blood stopped and the track fell into dense discussion with others and he, the yearling elk, was gone.

Sunlight for the low-angle sun filled in everything and then gave in to blue and below-zero again.

We broke a trail and did not speak, and we did not stop.

The cold followed us like sunlight follows shadows or precedes each blue shadow, waiting for its fall.

Goldfish

There's a warm spring where today people worry about meningitis,
   but when we were kids, people from town dumped unwanted
goldfish there, and sometimes a more exotic aquarium fish would
                              shimmer into our nets.

These days invasive bullfrogs gulp down everything they can but
   only within the melted confines adjacent to the bubble-up.

We netted a school of goldfish once, their scales already dingy or
fading from whatever it is that caused their brightness in the first
place and held the plastic sack full of them as if our hands waved
                  finlike through clear water all the way home.

Preparing for the transfer from baggie to bowl, I don't know
which of us spilled them, my ancestor, into the sink or which of us
        in our childish panic levered open the hot water valve.

                        The fish stilled just like that.

I think about our scramble of sun-warmed fingers and fish every
time I pass the warm spring on my way to go catch-and-release
                        fishing for cutthroat trout.

The places we love keep changing, their inhabitants, and we make
most of the changes without a thought to what we will make of the
new place, the inhabitants, ourselves in the place, ourselves after.

Common Sagebrush Lizard

We hunted the desert lizards while grandma gathered pine nuts
from the piñons along the roadside on the way to the lake.

She wore a red kerchief against the sun.

We burned.

We stayed, as best we could, in the shade between junipers and
pines.

My chosen weapon: a dart tipped with an orange rubber suction
cup that would, when sprung from its plastic gun, stick to glass if it
struck straight on, and if you hit a lizard just behind the head
sometimes the body would stun just long enough to snatch it up
and toss it into the red Folgers can with holes poked in the lid.

Once I missed ahead and one eye of that lizard bulged out dead:
the left eye that still looks at me sometimes in the summer crackle.

Ground Squirrel

Ten cents per tail was the bounty the owner of the pasture across
the highway offered you, my ancestor, so we hopped the wire
fence and hunkered down.

The summer air stank of balsamroot and brake pads burned during
someone's descent past our .22s toward their vacation in the valley
I still think of as ours.

We took aim at the holes mounded with dug dirt.

Wind noise and warning chirps.

Ricochets whined and little puffs of dust bloomed but nothing red
or twitching or still.

After we'd drunk all our Cokes, we took the hollow cans out with
us to inspect the mounds in case we'd missed a death along with
everything else, and we propped the cans as targets more or less
the size of the squirrels nobody could hit.

Both of us deadeyes with the cans; their red shine tumbling with
nearly every crack.

I miss the days in the dirt surrounded by no damage yet, just the
want to learn to cause some.

Ghosts

I thought the ghosts would come later, but, already, here they are,
my ancestor, between you and me.

For years, when I walked in the woods, when the dust tracked up
my legs, when the exhalations of plants and their flowers tendrilled
through my body, the ghosts of animals shadowed me.

Some I could identify as species: mule deer or black bear or ruffed
grouse, but then the ghosts came who were just the presence of
the lives here before our divisions and your lighting of flames.

The ghosts who followed me made no sound and had no eyes or
faces, and yet they took me in.

The lack in their voices was like an extinction or the passing of a
meteor.

The ghosts delivered no message, and I pricked my ears for none.

Of course, I was startled, but I sought no reason.

I came to expect the ghosts, even to long for them.

I stopped my habit of carrying flint and steel.

I became agreeable to most invitations that stayed below the treeline.

The animals came to me like a mist even as the glaciers above us dwindled to granite sepulchers, and I passed through the hot woods feeling my breath as a habitat for what were not things.

Mountain Lion

The lion crossed the dark highway lit by the beams I cast, the
beams we can't stop casting, into the darkness.

The lion tears across my vision still whenever I follow the highway
down to where it never ends in any place that is not awash in
unnecessary light.

The lion's body is still bright despite the bodies of useless mule
deer cast into the endless darkness by our endless need to race into
the night.

Moose

Paddling the placid thaw waters of the Oxbow, you and I saw beside the muck and quiet season a pale shape fiddlelike and risen as if an unexpected island.

We approached.

We found the body of a moose submerged except for the spinetrack, withers to rear, picked clear of hair, picked down to the white skin and the remainder of the animal body fully furred and fluid beneath the surface where perched carrion birds had not dipped their beaks.

We solemned as if passing a monument beyond what small waves count as history and into the terribly beautiful spring light of our passage toward a confluence of streams that grows still toward the Pacific, and how the pull of that paler night sphere makes of falling current another force, another irretrievable motion.

The joy we endured in a wild world unfettered by what we try to pin down or cast solid from fluid ore.

Golden Eagle

South of Cokeville the highway splits — left to Kemmerer and the
first JC Penney, right toward Randolph which calls itself the heart
of Utah (even though the town is just a few miles from the state
line) and is regularly the coldest town in that state where one river
system I stand in sometimes just wanders into the rabbitbrush
basins and dries up — at a place called Sage Junction (or at least
that's the name my family used even back when we met at the Red
Dog Saloon, so my sister and I would walk from one parent car to
another as if in some Cold War spy story except dusty instead of
billowed in mist) which is just down the state road from Sage
Creek Junction which is in Utah where my father lived not
Wyoming where I live still.

So you can imagine, my ancestor, precisely how I felt, years later
when — from how the meat of me hung from my bones — I was
clearly no longer a boy, and I flew up the grade at Sage Junction
toward the stop sign, watching a train on its track haul graffiti and
faraway and coal, and a golden eagle split the unbearable light and
nearly my windshield as it rose and rockered from a deer carcass to
updrafts to gone.

By now, you know the whole of me.

Mosquitos

So many bit me, I couldn't be bothered to bump or redden or itch.

That summer I bathed in the creek and grew willowlike, and my
blood went into the woods' wet hollows and spring sloughs.

My blood let clouds breed and fed bats and birds and trout;
sometimes I licked a cut.

The whine of their wings was nuisance enough, but we lasted
together in the cooling dusk and after the sun lifted mist from the
flesh of morning.

I planned meals and packed boxes of plain foods on the days I left
the camp and went to the school cabins all undermined by river
cobble and ground squirrels.

My only welt seared into my arm by a baking sheet too big for my
mitted fingers to grip.

I taught teens to cook plain foods and clean up without much
water and pack up what they didn't want the voles to forage.

Those unfamiliar kids stank of bug repellent.

I practiced feeding myself to the mud and what wings rose and bowed the quiet with filament wings nothing like swans or other angels.

Striped Skunk

The dead ones, roadside, lie flatted and smeared in this on-the-move season.

One I pass does not stink in the morning but then does in the afternoon.

One curls as if sleeping.

One day last week when I was again awake in the dark after a dream as forgettable as light, one must have shuffled past my window.

Its scent stung and faded.

I must have slept.

We had a dog when I was a boy who never learned to recoil from them, and was more than once sprayed and then sprayed again before wanting to be let in.

How, my ancestor, does one learn avoidance of a terrible gravitation?

I watch the world change and wonder what will pass the last time I breathe in.

Will it be black and white or parts of it red before not thinking?

Deer Mouse

The neighbor boys and I circled the water tank where the deer mouse circled within, its pelt blackened with damp to nearly the color of shrews and the smooth edge of the tank impossible to clamber up.

I was the first to dip my arm in to bridge a way out.

When I lifted my palm, the rodent bit my finger and leapt for the uncut grass around the fence buck base.

I bled.

I imagined needles in my belly.

My blood mixed with water raining the clover under me.

We had often rooted around in the midden stink of tumbledown cabins without the knowledge of what virus we might inhale, but none of us coughed, and none had become flesh to any mammal bite.

Another summer, years later, I woke in a field camp to a bucket left upright overnight and saw what was left of uncountable deer mice and what was left in the domed eyes of the cannibal survivor.

I feel the wounds every time in the woods, both those incisored into me and the carnage of which I am still the instigator by intent or accident and marked nonetheless.

Goshawk

Eurasian doves punctuated the chip seal expectedly.

Their steady coos and fluttering wings, the cough rattle of their
flapping woke us one summer and then for all summers until our
cul-de-sac sounds: lawnmowers, other engines idling spilled them
skyward.

The neighborhood always was a good place to learn about
expectations and evening.

Then — yes, you, my ancestor, knew there would be *then* — my
son saw, or I saw, a goshawk close enough for its red eye to
complement the quaking aspen roost where it watched for doves
to settle too long on the open pavement.

Some mornings the street wavered with feathers.

One morning I perched my son through the ending of what had
been our family.

We are gone from that place but not apart from what makes the
world patient, the wild patience that can be almost gentle like a
circle of red pierced by an opening into the inner perch.

Unknown

This side of a willowbreak I stumbled cobblebeds toward a seam in
the side-channel river flow where trout might feed.

I like being alone, and I was alone.

A chuff as if deep-chested shuffled willow leaves and my ease.

A word bigger than *go* from a mouth wet with wild crumbs of its
sustenance.

I was not alone and am never alone.

A hide-thick shape never snapped a branch as I broke back toward
the cutbank which gave the story of the river its binding, as if the
meat of me was safer when closer to the broken edge.

I trembled and waited for what might be just beside me to become
itself, a wild feeding, instead of wind in thin branches.

I am still becoming myself, my raw lung breath and eroded bones.

I tremble and wait.

Raven

My ancestor, you speak to ravens in their own language.

You are made up mostly of moose hair and snow.

You see a raven atop a blue spruce or within a web of cottonwood branches or just flapping overhead, and you begin to talk.

The raven answers, of course, for ravens were genial long before anyone attributed their words to somebody watching from a place above or below or unimaginably far.

After one winter storm, one raven told you how a pack of wolves had killed and eaten a moose down to less than bones.

You went together — my ancestor in your sealskin mukluks with soles gnawed by a grandmother and the raven with sharp-knapped obsidian wings — to take a look at what was left.

You arrived at the kill site just in time for the wind — the wind which kicks up like breath puffed from a dream whenever winter sunlight touches the late-morning drifts — to ruffle beard scruff and wings.

Even the magpies were through with the stain where the moose became meat.

You muttered, my ancestor, in the back of your throat, and the raven answered, a little call-and-response sounding nothing like a prayer, but exactly the way the run-off river whispers to the willow-softened bank.

You still will not say to me the words you spoke to the raven, but you swear the raven offered you its wings for your return across the undulating earth blanketed with mid-winter snow and weak light.

The light called — as light often calls in the wild places we prefer, my ancestor, to haunt — to the bone-gray moon tugging at the liquid surface of the world, as if calling somebody home.

Bison Calf

We worked the swale through summer heat, cranking a homemade
spool for barbed wire until our heads drummed.

This was the West and there was plenty of unnecessary wire to
tangle rusty ungulate legs in their unnoticing want to pass on to
another grassy place to bed down and later feed.

I drank little water as the hours coaled, and the drumming inside
my head grew into echoes of dry thunder.

I ate from sacks I'd stuffed into my backpack.

The line of posts hosted songbirds.

Where the cattle used to range, before feedlots and blame changed
another bad-luck economy, posts and wire then posts and a spool
then songbirds then on our way back to the trucks a band of bison
calves and a few unfettered mothers dipped their heavy heads to
graze.

In a day, we'd unmade a landscape (a term that was, you reminded
me the other day, itself not inhabiting our domestic interiors
before painters invented the word as they easeled their way
outdoors).

In a day, a landscape turned its wooly back on art and became what it always was, what I've always wanted and wanted to make, wild in its appearances and wild still in what does not appear.

I composed myself leaning on a top-rotten post.

Calves. Wind. Contrails.

Mottled Sculpin

A tributary river riffles into one of its green runs.

Cobbles mottle the bottom.

One fine-spotted cutthroat rises for a big fly, and when I reel it in,
half the body of a sculpin half-swallowed fills its mouth.

The sculpin's spines flare between a gulping and spitting out, and
yet still the trout tries to eat the hooked and gaudy lure I give it.

What to do with the flesh of a world of such gluttony but grab the
half-rotten tail of the sculpin in my pliers' hinge and pull it free.

Perhaps, my ancestor, I can release the living into its living.

The loose, dead flesh falls into the wash of water.

The hook curls free of the jaw, and the trout darts away to the
cutbank where insects dare the current's edge.

Later, I catch another meaty trout similarly stuffed and starving.

I regularly misplace the thought that I should drub a pan-sized fish
or two on a dry rock, carry those fresh carcasses home to cook.

I wake often in the run of night full of barbs and spines, my
stomach rumbling.

Bat

The first bat flapped around by the cabin hearth that my great-grandfather had built (as you know, my ancestor, we are not a family of builders) and where he got drunk with his fishing buddies who all looked like Norman Maclean.

You chased the bat with a net made to sling trout out from the slow river.

You were never swift or noticeably drunk before you were alone, but that night you leapt and swished the net to catch the bat, but then what?

How to release skin wings to the night was not like feeling fish slip into the starless water.

When, as a father, years later, I had a cabined bat, a son, and a wife I would later leave, we watched the dark shape tumble leaf-like near the inside peak of an A-frame.

We knew soon we would have to let it leave us, but first we watched it tumble leaf-like above us and the wood in the stove cracked and turned first to coals then ash.

When the time came for what indoors was tumbling and outdoors was night, we opened the cabin door, and something flew right out even as something else and more certain fluttered in.

I like to be out at dusk these days, sometimes knee-deep below a
riffle.

I like to be alone now and then and to get a little drunk.

I like my son a lot, how much he looks like his mother and how
much he is beginning to like to fish.

In spite and because of everything, my ancestor, I like you.

Just as the river becomes the sound of itself and the stars hatch, I
like to watch how winged the night might become and how young
I feel and how much like the old man I am stumbling to become.

Honeybee

Your hand in the clover lawn, pollen-skinned from the clumsy
stumbles of laden honeybees.

To say we knew the truth of species full in their intersections —
coat and pierce or something else as evidence of even fear as one
among our bloomings — would be a lie.

You simply held a body in your palm while I combed my still-soft
fingers under the green stems sending legs at their sweet work
tumbling down knucklebound.

Badger

Cobbled and damp-footed beside low river bluffs, I cast and
followed the drift over the speckled riverbed to the trundle of a
badger body downstream.

The rough of it and shag.

The way it forded the riffle and rifled the bank to divots and pits
and the tremble of ground squirrels and the echo of my often-late-
night mining for what doubt and shake burrow through me.

How unlike me and you, my ancestor, is this world: its course
grace in lazy summer hunts and little teardowns.

The convection wind drove only the reek of my own slakelessness,
unmasked by the careless way one body tore open the world,
found or did not find satisfaction, and left me unharmed and
alone.

How one wild thing never scars another in the same way we
discuss scarring.

My desire for wounds.

The thirst like gooseflesh.

Such a word: unsatisfied.

Rattlesnake

When I look up, I want to give up constellation patterns to the
light between voids.

The Milky Way is almost always not a tail thrashing the burlap dark
some amateur collector of reptiles dropped over while it dozed.

Even now, I want the gauze of the galaxy to knit the cuts from our
fine scalpels, but what washes over me has no point, is a current of
forces, is many currents shining under whichever light flickers
close or far from whichever fire.

Clouds have begun to gather in the orbs I call eyes.

Someday, I'll be on better terms with darkness, my ancestor, like
the rattlesnake I mistook for a dogstick and nearly grabbed in a
canyon mouth.

The whole grid of our ancestry fell before me.

The whole back of the snake bridged the arc I still refuse to touch.

Crow

We were almost to the lake before you, my ancestor, spoke in three
voices like a crow.

You claimed a raven spoke, but I saw the lesser shapes marionette
your lips and tongue.

One croaked with conviction about granite shoulders.

Another suspected snowbrush and smaller trees.

The third accused the lake of following a pattern scrawled in ice.

I watched the crows then confess lewdly to the sky.

As it was afternoon, the sky filled with its circumstance.

Behind the sky, another sky defamed the blue.

Its presumptions rumbled, as if glaciers still tilled the leftover
stones.

A hawk-black shape testified to lake-drowned snags festooned with
sticks of hellish compositions and tufted young waterfowl unable
yet to fly.

My ancestor, you said I should follow with open eyes upon open
rules.

Which voice within the voices you were speaking tweaked one
flight feather toward a gust of summer wind.

The untroubled lake remained clear enough for clouds to see
nearly to the darkest part and for that place to look up.

My ancestor, you kept muttering while I kept watch.

Cinnamon Teal

These quietest ducks quiet me in the green light of their early
nesting, before the last wastewater ponds I walk beside often and
through many weathers cover with algal blooms.

The teals are small.

Among cattails, teals can be difficult to notice.

The males dab not so much bright but aglow as if feathered in
willowstems.

Many smooth-barked shrubs glow all winter, freed for a season
from their plumage of leaves.

Each teal pair I see hovers my clumsy foot over one invisible nest
at the grass-riddled edge of Polecat Creek.

My gaze attended to the potential for dimples on the water surface
should trout begin to feed and not to the possible waterfowl
incubating under the crunch which was all that I was when my foot
came down.

There are days I do almost no damage that I notice.

There are days I hear no airplanes split the tidy sky into animals
and just us under the shadow footprints of clouds.

Cinnamon teals make themselves almost unnoticed.

I like them.

Bear

Lung bellows chuff behind a veil of willows.

My guts plunge deep in the slack tub.

The riverbed becomes the place where I am weak, where I am certain someone ursine can remake me.

Even the dry mud on the river stones falls silent.

I am away and alone without one guard hair to prove that the soundbody was, like mine, a body of coals and not a legion of devil regiments, of words in full retreat.

The animal time stills.

I am under its influence and the perfect clouds track an otherwise unmarked sky.

Sand Flea

Of the times I am an animal, I want now to tell you, my ancestor, this one: nineteen and outside a town stamped with a place name from old city where things happened which have stamped our ways of thinking, I camped at Two-Mile Lake (stamped with a name for the mileage from the trailhead, the point where you start and where you have to get back to if you want to get back to the house where you will imagine me living across the span of my sophomore college year and perhaps other houses where you have lived or where you now live or where you imagine I now live at this very moment alone).

In fact, my camp was not at Two-Mile Lake but on a dune above the tannic lake and old enough to not have a name and to hold a grove of small conifers and shrubs that hid my tent from no one (for in the days and nights I camped there I saw more seals than folks like me).

I watered at the lake and slept on the dune and, all of the rest of the time I was there, I stood or walked close to the surf.

Flat sand packed by waves, tossed around a bit by gusts from storms, and holed with homes for sand fleas which hopped (or did they scurry) as if animate sand.

Yes, there were seals, plentiful seals beyond the surf, and yes they watched me and we talked, but I much preferred the conversations I carried on with the indifferent fleas: how little they were, how little they had to say, how little their invisible wants, how their lives were just like my own life: small with a little home for a little while; both that home and this home, which is just my living body, made up mostly of water, air, and the same things as sand.

Coyote

One of the ways to make an American story a true story in a place with a little wild left, and increasingly, if the occasional report is accurate, also in cities and suburbs, is to add a coyote.

This story also includes a lab-mix leashed to a cabin, a willow break, a line of spruce trees named after a botanist from Frankfurt, and a summer evening.

My ancestor, picture the leash red.

Picture the dog agitated by yips from a solitary coyote on this side of a line of dark trees.

Picture the willow break in the evening light, a flat place not far from, but which, despite its flatness, bears little resemblance to, a parking lot, this lot for a trailhead to lakes named for a geologist and his subordinate who surveyed the place and tried and failed to summit the tallest peak, but nonetheless a lot alike to that parking lot outside Target, its red bullseye, or some such, the way a lab dog, a dull and pleasantly loyal animal, bears little in common, and yet still some connection, with the wild canine whining and yipping and held by sagebrush shadows and sere grass stalks and forbs.

Hear the coyote sounds as a beckoning.

The dog barks and tugs the red web taught.

Tags stamped with a name and address, proof of vaccination, clink and jingle without melody on the D-ringed collar clipped, you think securely, to the opposite of chasing.

Beyond the line of Engelmanns, picture eyes and muzzles of an unspecified pack number but plenty to rend the pet should the tether fail.

The lone as bait, and the rest as switch.

The change to night is often an easy breeze stirring each willow leaf.

Now you are yourself again making your way home to the cul-de-sac, your ragged garden, your interiors.

Red-winged Blackbird

The kindness of blackbirds returns red-shouldered before the
cattails sprout, when the muck which is their country twitches
under snow and ice crystal snares.

I was a boy in these places, and I never feared the hunger of
badger holes or of the sky.

Yes, my ancestor, there were storms we avoided and those we did
not, the shames of our flesh and the shamelessness.

The leeches in the pasture ponds became our limbs or the silt we
stirred up.

We crawled among the willow woods alone and together.

Sometimes we were fully clothed.

We tore apart grasshoppers and sucked at stems until we too gave
up green.

We built gestures out of mud, but they refused to tremble along
beside us.

Once, I fled to the far edge of the world steaming from the bath
with just a blanket and the night before me.

Crouched among the benign cobbles, my breath ran on.

I imagined myself alone.

Of course, lightning flared, and vapor spoke to vapor.

Other than the sky, the voices were silt-spattered and small.

Even the frogs refused to shout back, and the cattails and catkins
stilled.

I held that part of me that never quite returns from its travels like
the shrew you never would have rescued from the stock tank, that
shrew that drew blood from my pointer finger.

I made a shelter of my palms, and a heat found its den there.

That night had already recollected how the frost would play with
patterns so small as to seem invisible and unimportant, how
another frost would creep up what stalks it could reach to bloom.

The whole earth knew I would go back into the log house where
my family shone dimly before the fullness of dark, but no part of
the winded world left me with any kind of debt.

Another kindness in a pasture alive with kindnesses.

I have made my attempts to separate myself from what tangles, my
ancestor, but now I sign my oaths with a bone from a wing.

PLANT APPARITIONS

Observe, my ancestor, white   blossoms as columbine.
Report the columbine   above the ripening
whortleberries. Presume   red tendrils back
to the red of fruiting   bodies. Examine the red
stain of the plucked   fruit. Quarrel fingertips,
your convictions. Suspect   the family of fruiting
bodies. Leave the beetle   to its mark. Utter
the contractions of these   unfamiliar textures.
Prove flavor by baring   teeth. Scratch the weak
dew from the knuckle   edge. Give testimony
which is also oath-moan.   Dye cell by cell
to the fleeting flavor.   Confess to finish
or further the inquiry.   Witness the uselessness
of cuspids in the acquisition   of language or
of flavor. Call upon   the league of leaves,
their hidden reddening.   Entertain the familiar
beetle fingering a fingernail.   Divine the passage
of the black beetle   into nearby blackness,
unwarranted red,   token red, signal red,
faltering, forsaking,   confessing, gesturing,
pranking, malignant red,   circumstantial red,
what has been called   the witches' mark,
the witches' words,   the witches' deeds,
the witches' ecstasies.   Witnesses the witches'
confessions, as you have   long done, my ancestor,

as if white flowers   aching always lightward.

Maybe in that late day   a flame or shadow
darted into me. The tree   coaled beneath itself
with spent needles. Late   August exhaled. I was
a breathing boy still   looking forward to light
as much as fading. I was   beginning a year,
and I was familiar   with sorceries. To this
day, I see things I can't   explain and don't
bother trying. I still   sit in the dirt with my
hands. The world goes on   whispering just out
of earshot and the crick   in my neck from listening.
I watch the needles pile   up and feel them brush
shoulders of the moraine.   Dirt will hold me
on the last day and dirt   will also hold me after.

I had not been seen   by stems back then,
but I had tasted them,   and I had cut them
down. Hungry for sweeter   veins of the woods,
I plucked and sipped   grasses, popped clover-
heads, buggy and full,   into my boymouth
for the flood of crushed   cells. Among ghost
shadows of summer pines   I extracted the flutes
of columbine one at a time   to nip the slim tip
and let what sweet they kept   for hawkmoths,
which look like hummingbirds   among the mottled
shadows of summer pines,   roll sweetly down
my tongue's spine. Time   passed, and more of me

grew barked and galled.   I grew into my fragile
hungers, and I knew   how to hold their dusted
pulse. The white flowers   looked less and less
        like secret treats and more   like little wings
of a stillness I reached for   without talons or clutch.

        I didn't know poison ivy   grew along the red
        rock canyon stream   until I stood knee-deep
    in its red stems, or that   such a thing as bighorn
    sheep lived anywhere   except carved into some
        canyon wall until the rams   and ewes stood all
around me. When my legs   began to burn and blister
        I waded crotch-deep   into the canyon stream
        to let the water calm me.   I didn't know that
    standing in any wild place   I'd never before been
        could feel like anything   but lust. I still don't
know any other feeling.   Those parts of my animal
body that can only be called   flanks quiver and itch,
        and whatever live skin   brushes my live skin
        welts me as I slip   through folds of leaves
        toward the cold tug   of clear water. I fished
        for trout in the deep   pools. Trout raised
    in a hatchery cinder-   blocked around the spring
        that fed the tanks full   of fry and couldn't help
        itself but pour toward   the ocean-bound.
    The later river, I have   read, no longer rushes
    with any urgency   toward the hips of the sea.

A fragment of some   forgotten stone lodged
in my right-hand, pointer-   finger, fist knuckle
after I struck the pre-   shattered rock a splitting
blow from a hammer   no one in our cabin house
minded that I used   for my rockhounding.
I don't remember goggles   or glasses, so what
became part of me could   have been worse. That
was a boyhood time when   my boyself cottonwooded.
Now, in this later, too-   warm summer, a leaf
prickle from a Canada   thistle lances my opposing
thumb and leaves its initial   pierce inside, I believe,
the meat of me. It throbs   when I worry the mark
it made, but I do not call   my doctor, who was
a neighbor in the rock-   smacking days, to have
him cut it away. I grow   neither leaf-like nor
calcified in what has come   to resemble a tumble
of seasons. I fill up, digit   by digit, with shards,
the piles of sharp ends   of the left-unclobbered
wild, and I try not to let go   of their not letting me go.

Fall hawthorn branches   laden with waxwings
and hard fruit of skin-   gripped seeds. Sunup
thorns sting the frost-   laden arc. Every flutter
of my wicked cells   in mourning. One at a time
the flocks go a little   farther toward away
to that dull place   beyond place where nothing
but what you, my ancestor,   say is blessed ripens
around a seed loosed   leathery and groundward.

70

We often gorged   among the hackled branches
        near tumult streams.   Our world was plain
        as granite scree.   What was familiar was sad
        people and the slow   erosion of sad people.
        I would come to know   sandstone, tamarisk
        throat-handing desert   streams, and a woman
invaded by weeds; and you,   my ancestor, would
        familiarize yourself   with techniques to carry
    a car-wrecked girl away   from Montana before
the highway patrol arrived.   But in our teens, we knew
        only that altitude was red   and seedy and tasted
    like shards where marmots   perched in our Augusts.
        Years later, we tried   to fall in love or to act
        at last on the years   of falling, but for a couple
    of lean-bodied summers   you and I did not need
    the simple sadness of two   bodies squeezed into one
        clutch. We knew which   red fruit we could pull
    from brambles and swallow,   and which harvests
among summer's profusions   would poison or prick us.

        I have twinged, cactus   spines hooked in my skin,
            severally: looking away   from a windowsill
        pot, pulling a bulb   from the white dog's leg
        before he could chew it,   brushing against what
            the dog missed, so on.   Never have I known
    thirst like the lost throat   of a vast place that I did
        not think was meant   for my voice or safe,

71

even when not-for-   certain safe. This calloused
luck of my ancestry,   its inevitable cruelty.

Before I knew henbane   was an invasive plant
where I live, I thought   the speckled flowers
were beautiful. After?   Still. Before I knew
how toxic henbane   could be in all its parts
to the heart, I let stalks   flourish in my yard,
admired the blossoms   adorning the space
above the array of leaves.   Once I knew henbane
was invasive, I released   roots from the dirt
with a firm tug. I may   have touched some
plants with bare hands.   I may have feared
that you, ancestor, brushed   your toddler fingers
over the mottled petals.   Once I knew that
henbane was long used   either as medicine
or hallucinogen, I thought   about times the world
seemed strange to me,   like how stars revealed
their varying distances   from my pinpoint vision,
even those long since   coaled to emptiness,
and I was unaffected.   I like pilsner in the summer,
but sometimes one   slurs me. Sometimes, I think
my thoughts are toxic,   but that has yet to stop me
from thinking or feeling   gratitude for you alive
still in this unfamiliar world,   a feeling like a branch-
tossing gust as it gathers   leaves before a cold front.
And I can't help but reach   out to what grows.

Pasture willows grew   into hovels we entered
    and sat surrounded   by stick walls. We knew,
my ancestor, others   who needed shelter: the boy
    whose dad chased us   off if we came near
    his son while his son   trembled, the boy
    whose dad we never saw   but about whom
    our parents whispered,   the boys at the end
of the lane whose grandmother   stabbed a shotgun
at them from her porch   when they strayed
        into her drunken yard.   We were almost
fatherless and often   happy and without reason
    to fear what our parents   could do beyond
    their falling silent   and into separate rooms.
        We grew woody   and leaved, muddy
and trailing dried algae   strands, ripe, my ancestor,
    with the must   of willow bark. We emerged
festooned with the half-   wildness of the pasture,
    and sheltered by the gray   hands of branches.

    I irrigated the steer field   the summer before
        middle school. If you   were not picked up
    by dusk, then you biked   with me and hauled
    the thin timbers and orange   tarps with me, lifted
    river stones to weight   the tarps to keep them
    from billowing away   like water, and the work
    went faster. So, we'd linger.   Once, a town kid
    slithered under the low   strand of barbed wire
    instead of scaling it,   ladder-like near the staple

in a grounded post,   and you laughed, my ancestor,
instead of showing him   our way. He rose, forearms
   sliced from the sedges,   apart from the rest of us
      and giggling. That fall   in town, we would feel
like difference. Some nights   the dusk surrounded
      us. In the field, the steers   followed in groups,
emboldened each other   to snort and false charge
   until we spun and flung   our sunburned arms
upward and woofed. They   would always spook,
   the steers, and the ones   that had been bravest
would lead their scared leaps   backward. We were
      already well aware   of following and leading.
   If the steers butted heads   in flight from us,
we chucked each other   fist to shoulder. The ride
   home was always straight   into a darkening.

      My heartbeat begins   to feel like not-a-heart
      when I have gone   a time without the river
      pulsing strong around   my body. In such
      seasons, the little   houndstooth fist I pull
         from a sock or sleeve   and pinch until
   it holds my thumb   or pointer finger is like
   the river's reprieve   as its own heart-shaped
glacier diminishes, seems   to recharge among
the accumulation of storms   only to diminish
      in another dull throb   of summer days.
         What a lost pair   of words: *my body*.
      As if anything is split   or otherwise held.

As if the nature   of holding is anything
other than holding   and then again holding.

Allergies for years   would make you think,
my ancestor, that I should   avoid goldenrod
in bloom, but bees   and summer heat, the muddy
mistbreath of pasture   and the weedy edges
of rural roads before   the sere clung to my body
(such a sad bumble   of tongues to call this
"mine") the way hooked   ends of grasshopper
legs drew carapace   to boy skin. I leaned
and lean in. The sun once   blistered my shoulders,
left me wheezy and   flattened on the couch
while you, ancestor, went   off to some shaded place
I can't remember.   Sunstroked, I slept, and if
I were to say that   in my sleep I found myself
in a field of goldenrod,   then already now my eyes
burn at the thought   of a clear-lunged summer
without horses or idle   gravel-kicking where roadcut
goldenrod hummed   and I drummed inside
myself like pollen thunders   in clumps on the last
legs of bees. Bees I rarely   see now outside
mismatched hive boxes   hemmed by crops
when I am outside   with a task or two, a purpose
that, unlike fever dreams   of a boy never learning
how to be a man or even   manchild, is of no use
to this weedy world   other than exhalation.
The way I know my self-   deception is the lie

divided into my body   and all the other wildlife.

The other day, I talked   to a tree, a spruce
robed in black for the short   month with heavy
snow. The tree grew   in my neighbor's yard,
and had been doing so   for long enough to have
been brushed by the same   winds that once brushed
the spruces in my yard,   the trees my friend
cut down. I was glad   that you, my ancestor,
were in your moldering   place away on a far hill,
because I spoke aloud   to the tree, and I knew
what you would think   of that. Nothing sinister,
just a little chit-chat   about the tricks the tree
was eager to perfect.   You see, the spruce was
teaching other trees   even the disheveled
birch and the graceful,   albeit shabby, golden
willow, a little sleight-   of-hand magic. The spruce
held snow and then   gone, just like that, gone.
The snow was gone   just like that. The branches
that had held the snow   only a moment before
wavered as if brushed   by a summer wind. I watched
closely. I listened   for the snow to murmur
as it fell or when it landed.   I was impressed
with how silently the snow   slipped past the many
hands of the spruce. Who   wouldn't feel compelled
to admire a magician   for such a trick, and so
I spoke. The dogs listened   to me congratulating
the spruce tree instead   of their neighbor's barks.

The other trees clapped,   letting all of the snow
     they had held onto   fall back to the same
old earth you, my ancestor,   still molder under far
     off in your stone cloak   and hat. I have not said
     one word of this account   of tree magic aloud
to you, just tick, tick,   tick. But now let's speak
     into each other's ears   in whispers or what is
left. You don't need to be   afraid of what I want
to tell you. Maybe those   spells you spoke fear into
carried you off into your   wicked brand of thought,
     but the earth is where   I never want my bones
     to leave, the dirt where   even your bones
     are still tucked up   some other place's sleeve.

     Nearly thirty species   of willows inhabit
          the drainage of a river   I like to fish,
     and some of these   species hold me.
     Moose and cattle   wend mazes through
     the overlap of stalks,   and I follow them.
     Once in a while, I spook   this or that calf
     or a crashing. Some paths   end, and I try
     to make my own way   twisting or ducking
     until I am stuck fast   and laugh. I'm slapped
     or my waders pierced   by a sprung branch
     of a willow I can't pick   out from a species list
     or don't bother. The species   grow side-by-side
     in varied greens. I'd like   to make a connection.
     Their barks turn subtle   winter colors once

their yellow leaves   are lost to them (Or should
I say, *let go*, my ancestor?).   From far off, their colors
ease my way through another   icy, troutless season.
I find it difficult to reverse   course, to backtrack
instead of china-shopping   forward into thickets.
I'm not so different from men   like you, my ancestor,
who I see and have seen   believe freedom is sticking
to whatever I want or say   or do all on my own.

Trailside, wild strawberries   taste, you said, like clouds
as we fondled our way   under leaves to pluck
them. You, in keeping, ate   as many as were ripe
for your fingers, and I,   in keeping, ate only
a few, thinking that less   would make the flavor
linger, first on my tongue   and after the memory.
You fell in love with a dying   man years before you
met me. I was married   for as many seasons
as I was not, and then   I was not. You told me
you would always love   him, and I stumbled
to make tendril room.I let   go of a life, my ancestor,
and sometimes crushed   its fruit. What I did
not say on the dappled   slopes on the way
to a place that would be   just ours but was not
yet, is that you knew   more about the woods
and what to do in them   than I knew, and that
the story of one life   made out of two
is easier to tell when each   page before the end
can be touched, the last   words are already inked.

Clouds built up and fell   apart, like the fruit
in our mouths, sweet   and like everything.

My thumbnail moonshell   knifes treeskin
and douses my knuckle   with sap like turpentine.
This pungent blood   of these elegant trees
carries groundfire embers   into the canopy, lets
the summer's whisper   smolder-yelp its catastrophe.
I can't stop piercing   bark, rubbing the current
of nourishing into me.   The forest is phoenix
and I have been one   among the grounded
to watch or flee.   I'll never testify
for the prosecution, even   if my judgment won't
wash off of me. Sap   sticks, yes, and I want,
my ancestor, the sharpness   of the fir's desire
to cling, my ancestor,   like soot in dirt, to me.

I have awakened   with such heat for the wild
world growling in me   that I have sprung
from shelter to enter   the first dense bramble
I could. I have felt   myself muddy to swell
and spill into the green   world erect and waving
to receive me. Even   as I gray, I feel the rut
in me among bark folds   and downdrafts, the throb
in buds and ticklish   catkins. I have made
of my pulse a vessel   for moan. I have pricked
my ears to what wild   is left moaning back.
I have felt the duff dig   into my shoulder blades

79

and how each little   death is also never dying.

When I part from the trail,   flowers and stalks
cover the bare skin   of my walking in a film.
    The residue snares   dust and seeds.
    Sometimes ants and ticks   stick to the scum
which covers me. I stink   of geranium musk
        when I come back   to the bloomless lot.
I reek of the dust   and like their petals
        my skin too blushes   under the thirsty
sun. The trail runs   beside the bottom
        of the fault, runs   alongside the stream
        carving the edge   of the lot, lies
        alongside a larger   stream. I mean
to say I am not ignorant   to the entanglements
I seek, my ancestor,   on every side of where
        I should be, where   you want me to write
        my letters with fingers   rather than feet.

    Enchantment fell away   under an evening
    fir. I remember the red   August and the soft
    needles. Grasses spread   abroad and golden
with seedheads. Stalks   and stems and the sweat
    of geraniums sticking   the air together. I knew
that place and its shadow   where I would see
into my days, and I gave   no fear to the horizon
beyond the dusk of my birth.   I was neither prey
nor did I genuflect. I felt   my skin-warmth mingle

with the flesh of the pebbled   earth. None of this
was an awakening   nor an arousal. I simply held
        onto a body of loam   which was my own,
          my voluntary exile   in the squalid desert
          that is the sole place   my abominable self,
which is all there is of me,   which has escaped
the links of your voice,   my ancestor, your bombast,
and our twining code.   I struggle to seek bedrest
        under the gift of duff   not your cruel vellum.

Following a spring creek   toward the muddy river,
I passed through a patch   of poison ivy before you
pointed it out to me.   The day went on warming.
Tamarisks pelted the banks.   Bighorns remained,
        like the silent vipers,   translucent. I stood
        in the water some   and sometimes I hiked
against the current spooking   trout from one red
sandstone bowl to another.   I caught a few fish
        before the rest darted   away from my skin
        and the irritant fading   from me. My body
burned a little and then   stopped burning. I itched
        a bit, but the underground   water soothed me
        even after it bubbled up   inside a corrugated
hatchery before tumbling   into the open, even if
I soothed not one wild   witness of my passage.

My ancestor, you docked the red   boat while I brought
        out our stringered catch.   Your request for me

to clean the fish for our   dinner felt not quite
question or command.   You shut the cabin door
to me, and the evening   went on. I lined each
dry-eyed fish just so   in the stubbled grass
and clover weeds. I checked   the cabin window
before plucking dandelions   to place just so
between one once-silver   fish and the next. I had
not gutted fish in years,   but, like all small brutalities,
the simplicity came back   to me as if staining
my knifeblade. I bade each   fish farewell as if they
were not, the lot of them,   already gone. Quite
quiet and ceremonial,   I pulled inside from outside
to the newspaper   and dandelion blooms. You
rinsed each piscine streak   of meat in the spigot sink,
patted dry the skin, lay   each in the pan with sliced
onion. We ate into the silent   summer night and,
after, nothing dared   to dart through my dreams.

We prized the cones   fallen from subalpine
firs as ammunition   which was the same
as currency for our   childhood wars. The strobiles
were hard and hurt   in the way we wanted,
my ancestor, to be hurt,   stung in the way we wanted
our bodies and each   other's bodies to sting.
When you sprinted   for the boards laddered
up to the platform piled   with projectiles to augment
your pocketfuls, the game   turned, and I turned
against you, the runner,   my ancestor, aiming whatever

cones I could grab and chuck   at you. On occasion,
     a rock may have been thrown.   If you made it
     to the platform perch,   my ancestor, hitting me
     was easy, and so you   lessoned me something
about how power works,   but eventually you had
     to come down and be   welted. I did not yet
know that subalpine firs   bleed sap like turpentine,
and when wildfires spark   that liquid fire introduces
     the canopy to flame.   The world is still like this:
     hard with sheltered seeds   and ready to burn.
We are as we were: playing   at war as if dodging
     consequence with our back   pocket matchbooks
from the Stagecoach Bar   already full of those struck.

     There is nothing much   to the hawthorn berry:
     leathery skin stretched   over a pit. That's about it.
     And thorns at least an inch   long along each stem
     and strong enough to pierce   through the sole
of a boot, my ancestor. Berries   a deeper shade of bark
shaded by almost autumn   leaves. And yet, black bears
     lean their limbs into thinning   hawthorn branches
     to gorge. Bear scat pebbled   with pits and scraps
of skin. And the time I stood   between a bear stripping
     a hawthorn bare and a few   people peering nearer
     to him. And then that other   time outside a plank-
floored place when the whole   downtown profusion
     of spike-branched limbs   transformed into flocks
     of cedar waxwings, so many   their waxy bands

83

of yellow and red thorned   the berried twigs. I live
in a town where wild things   invite themselves in
so often they often go   unnoticed for being so
unrare. I live in a place   where I have gorged myself
on bear meat sausage   and where I have heard
firsthand that men look   almost like bears once
bears have lost the thin   trappings of their bearlike
skin. I am profuse with how   I am thin-skinned
and how I think of my bones   as thin. And, my ancestor,
how thornlike our colors   and claws have always been.

Yes, I have boiled nettles   in a camp pot to eat
and called them sour   and compared them to this
or that leaf picked up   at the grocery store
in the humdrum summer   heat and tourist haze.
Yes, I have leaned my leg   into them to be stung,
if only for the sake   of feeling. I have carried
chosen pains and those   stumbled through all day
and let them welt   and redden me. Yes, I have
stood wincing in a stream   beside festooning nettles.
I have allowed myself   to go all numb, my ancestor,
beyond the simple pain   of feeling what nourishes.

I returned from searching   for the next plot
metered ten-by-ten   where two years prior fire
deviled everything   to pebbled dirt and black.
My job to lead a group   of students from square
to square to count what   new grew there: trees,

forbs and grasses. Heat   cicada-buzzed me quiet,
the group quiet, stalked   between boy-high stems
of fireweed. the bloom-   stalks like cairns covered
in pink butterflies. My eyes   unable to find anyone
in the world talling back   into itself, rooted in black
release of what it takes   to root again. Clouds piled
up as they might have   when the strike caught.
No one spoke and I could   not find them. My steps
crushed one or another   plant. I parted greenly
into the circle of young   hands sticky with fireweed
reek and feathered   by wisps of seeds like words
I could not speak, have   not yet learned to speak,
my ancestor, outside this   voice I use to speak to you.

Neither of us ever fought   in a war that was not
playing at war as boys   before we met and became
friends who never fought.   The wars I played at
were with boys I knew   and usually included
melting plastic army men   or lighting the fuses
of as many bottle rockets   as we could tape or tie
to try to launch the men   we had not melted
into the street. The wars   you played at were not
anything we talked about.   The river called and
sometimes we answered   together, like the time
before my marriage ended   in a peaceful accord
when a storm sprung up   no more quickly than any
other August afternoon   but quick enough and with
enough charge crackling   through it that we had

85

to hustle from the side   channel toward the car.
You never liked lightning   or thunder. You never
liked to show how scared   you were of air, so we fled
into the cottonwood grove   dappled with already-
fallen leaves and sunlight   and elk bones. We hustled
and lowered our rods   and watched the hairs
on our arms for the terror   of standing. And just like
that the trees show-curtained   onto a river channel
facing the stormlit peaks   I had lived near for years
and just then did not know,   the same channel we had
left minutes before.   We were together, my ancestor,
when inattention to the line   between place and thought
in fear of a bolt were a circle   we looped before any rain.
I was with you once   when you killed an elk
and once when we tracked   one wounded through
a long, cold day. Apart   when you watched a man
breathe in the river   and when I kindled
my partnered life to ash   before replanting. You
have lost more people   you love than I have lost,
my ancestor, and someday   I will die and you
will stand and turn   under leaflight, under bark
scars, and there will be   a war someplace we will
not visit and I hope   my son will not be there.
I wonder, my ancestor,   will you remark on how
the river channels are dry   where they used to be.

This time, the extinction   event is profusion
and black bear shit-slurry   worrying the trail.

Fingerling branches bow   with berryweight before
    teeth and lips strip them   nearly bare. If I am
not taking off my clothes   in the woods, then I am
    thinking about disrobing   and the bright pricks
        of frost or sunlight   honing me. Off trail,
        the rivulet loudens,   and the maze of things
presents itself as shadows   beyond each selection.
I am one of those people   who was told, "Turn
    right. Turn right. Turn   right." I have heard
that fruit sweetens after   a hard frost. My body,
    as do bodies, stiffens   and softens. The crush
    of seedflesh in my mouth   bitters me inside
as if dust. I have fallen   face-first into clawmarks
on the coated skins   of aspens. Broken-branch
        scars eye me or flit   away like waxwings.
Some birds become   so much fermented fruit
    they lose the will   to flight. Some bears reach
    past shambled wasp   nests and tug the fine
    branches mouthward.   I have been talking
with my bare tongue   about the speechless places.
    I have felt their tang fall,   like a spider thread,
into my belly. Some cubs   let the profusion of fine
    twigs hold them until all   the fruits are pits.
    Snow will clamp down   and after that, sprouts.

I keep telling this story   and yet I cannot identify
    the species of needled tree   I prepared to live
    my life under. You are,   by now, familiar

with the details: child,   birthday, trail, two lakes,
excitement into a dash   up the wrong trail, tall
grass, red needles, evening,   solitude. I do not
remember loving or even   reading stories of boys
lost in wild places or raised   by wild mothers.
Instead, I liked the one   about the boy who flew
an airplane made of bread   dough. I never cared
where he landed. I know   that I felt, whether
or not this really happened,   as if I could become
this ragged life raised   by a conifer I still cannot
name, raised on a green   slope punctuated by forbs
under branch shadow   and comforted by the red-
needled duff and cones.   I sense now, with that sense
underneath my senses,   how some new self
birthed itself that day,   how quiet I could be,
and how you, my ancestor,   with your unusual name
called out my plain   name over the slope
of plants just tall enough   to hold me out of sight,
and how my tongue   spoke the language of bark
instead of tumbling   into your arms. Even that young,
I knew what I would always   be leaving. I have
known other women   and men, other forests
with their many trees,   and I have felt in myself
your ancient feeling: disappointment and,
underneath, my ancestor,   the pulsing of sap.

I will not stop giving   myself bodily to
the meadow. Stems   of alpine timothy bend

under me in their ancient   way of offering
    to spring back up   as soon as I go on.
I have no memories   of a mouth that did not
    sip from culms. One   of these days, I'll be
underground or sprinkled   over a field in flower
or a field of snow   or planted with the roots
    of a little tree ready   to embrace everything
    but the metal bits   of me, the mercury
and screws. To be made   again of sunlight
and the reachings   of radicles is the oldest
    memory I've written   into each place
I've touched and every   touching part of me.
Oh, to reek of earth again   and to be unconcerned
    with patterns made   of stars or words

ABOUT THE AUTHOR

Matt Daly is the author of the poetry collection, *Between Here and Home* (Unsolicited Press), and the chapbook, *Red State* (Seven Kitchens Press). He is the recipient of a Neltje Blanchan Award for writing inspired by the natural world and a Creative Writing Fellowship in Poetry from the Wyoming Arts Council. He lives in Wyoming.

ABOUT THE PRESS

Unsolicited Press is based out of Portland, Oregon and focuses on the works of the unsung and underrepresented. As a womxn-owned, all-volunteer small publisher that doesn't worry about profits as much as championing exceptional literature, we have the privilege of partnering with authors skirting the fringes of the lit world. We've worked with emerging and award-winning authors such as Shann Ray, Anthony DiPietro, Amy Shimshon-Santo, Brook Bhagat, Kris Amos, Amy Baskin, and John W. Bateman.

Learn more at unsolicitedpress.com. Find us on twitter and instagram.